Tayta Remembers

AMAL ABOU-EID & CARA KING

For my grandparents - May your stories never be forgotten. AA

To my family, Pete, Charlie and Angus, with love. CK

First published by Amal Abou-Eid 2021
www.booksbyamal.com.au

Copyright © 2021 in text: Amal Abou-Eid
and illustrations: Cara King

National Library of Australia
Cataloguing-in-Publication entry:
ISBN: 978-0-6487113-2-2
Designed by Cara King
www.caratoons.com
Printed by Ingram Spark

Tayta
Remembers

Sunday mornings are special mornings.
Sunday breakfast is the best breakfast.

On Sundays, Tayta prepares a traditional breakfast for her family. She wakes up early to prepare the dough. It needs plenty of time to rest.

Adam leaps out of bed and gets ready in a hurry.
He loves Sunday mornings.
He loves Tayta's breakfast.

Baba plays old Arabic songs in the car. He hums along to songs about love, hopes and dreams. Mama sways and hums along, too. 'We danced to this song on our wedding day,' she tells Adam.

The scent of freshly baked
biscuits fills the air.
Adam's senses tingle.

'I'm here!' he shouts, as he
enters the house. The door is
never locked at Tayta's house.

'*Ahla habibi*. I made your favourite *kaak*,' whispers Tayta and gives him the tightest hug.

Adam spots a broom in the corner and rides it like a horse.
'Giddy up horsey, giddy up!'

Tayta watches him and smiles. She remembers riding her father's horse around the village in Lebanon, the autumn wind in her hair and thick mud on her boots.

Mama uncovers the balls of dough Tayta prepared for
the *manakish*. She rolls them out into flat discs and
tops them with *zaatar*, cheese and meat.

Tayta loved helping her mother roll out dough. Together, they cooked the yummiest **manakish** and fed everyone in their village.

Baba pops open jars of *zaytoun* and pickled vegetables.
He scoops some out and puts them into small bowls.

Memories of long days spent at **karm al-zaytoun** fill
Tayta's mind. Young men tapped the trees above;
zaytoun fell to the ground. '**Zaytoun** is a blessed fruit,'
her father would say, as they gathered them all up.

Adam gallops between rows of cucumbers and tomatoes in the garden. 'Don't step on the mint and parsley!' calls Jeddo.

Tayta smiles as she remembers her mother picking
bunches of herbs from the garden. She made fresh mint
tea in the afternoons as she listened to the songs of the birds.

'Pick some lemons for the *ful mudammas*,' says Tayta.

'Can we make lemonade, too?' asks Adam.

'Of course we can, *habibi*,' replies Tayta.

She thinks of the large trees in her father's **bustaan**.
Apple trees, fig trees and a vineyard full of the juiciest
grapes. Summer was delicious in the village.

The **saaj** is hot and ready. Tayta whacks the dough, flips it and twirls it. She bakes fresh **khobz** and **manakish** on her dome shaped oven.

The slap and the sizzle bring back memories of
the *tannour* in the village. Young women chatted and
laughed as they stood around the *tannour*, baking fresh
khobz for their families.

'Your apron is covered in flour,' says Adam, as he sneaks up to eat some **khobz**.

'You can make a lot of delicious food with flour,' says Tayta.

Tayta remembers her father working in the golden fields, gathering wheat and sorting grains. He took sacks of dried grains to the miller and returned home with bags of flour.

Jeddo fries some eggs, sunny-side up, and boils a big pot of black tea. 'Nearly done,' he says, as he adds sugar to the teapot.

The big pot of tea reminds Tayta of the cold winter months in the village. She spent many nights, around the hot coal heater with her family, roasting chestnuts and telling stories.

'*Yallah* Adam, get the milk from the fridge and help set the table,' says Mama, as she spreads the *labneh* onto flat plates.

Tayta remembers the old dairy cow in the village. Her mother milked her twice a day. She churned the milk to make butter, strained the yoghurt to make *labneh* and sun-dried the cheese to make *shanklish*.

Mama squeezes lemon juice over the mashed *ful mudammas* and mixes it all together. She separates it into bowls and drizzles olive oil on top.

Tayta grins as she thinks of her father's stalks of corn, fava beans and barley. She loved watching the clouds pass by, as she hid amongst the leaves and enjoyed the warm spring sun.

Breakfast is ready!

Adam licks his lips and rubs his tummy. 'This is the best food in the whole world!' he says, with an enormous smile on his face.

'I used to say the same thing to my mama,' says Tayta, delighted by the memories of her childhood and her homeland.

GLOSSARY

Ahla: welcome/hello

Baba: Father/Dad

Bustaan: orchard/garden

Ful mudammas: boiled dried fava beans often mixed with lemon and garlic

Habibi: my love/term of endearment

Jeddo: Grandfather

Kaak: traditional Lebanese biscuits

Karm al-zaytoun: olive grove

Khobz: Lebanese flatbread

Labneh: strained yogurt

Mama: Mother/Mum

Manakish: Lebanese bread topped with a variety of toppings and fillings

Saaj: a dome shaped metal cooktop with a heat source underneath it

Shanklish: aged fermented cheese made from yoghurt whey, usually covered in thyme, zaatar or chilli

Tannour: a cylindrical clay oven that retains heat, commonly shared by multiple families within an area

Tayta: Grandmother

Yallah: hurry up/quickly

Zaatar: a combination of herbs, sesame seeds and sumac

Zaytoun: olives

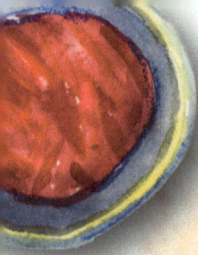

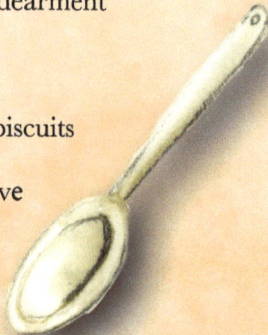

www.ingramcontent.com/pod-product-compliance
Lightning Source LLC
Chambersburg PA
CBHW042026090426

42811CB00016B/1754